If I Be Lifted Up

Reflections for the Season of Lent

by
George Lacey, O.S.B.

PAULIST PRESS
New York / Mahwah, N.J.

Cover design by Frank Vitale

Library of Congress Cataloging-in-Publication Data

Lacey, George, 1932–
    If I be lifted up : reflections for the season of Lent / by George Lacey.
        p.   cm.
    ISBN 0-8091-3761-5 (alk. paper)
    1. Lent—Prayer-books and devotions—English. I. Title.
BX2170.L4L   1997
242'.34—dc21   97-22788
                                                                    CIP

Published by Paulist Press
997 Macarthur Boulevard
Mahwah, New Jersey 07430

Printed and bound in the
United States of America

Foreword

These readings can be used in several ways. Based largely on the gospel of the day, they can be used for brief homilies at the daily masses during Lent. (The readings for the Sundays follow year A; although those of the first Sunday of Lent, the temptations of Christ, occur in B and C also.) They can also be used as readings for the daily divine office, whether in the morning or evening. Or they can be used for what they are primarily intended, that is, as daily reflections for the season of Lent based upon the liturgical readings.

Special thanks are due to Donald F. Brophy, the managing editor of the Paulist Press, and his staff, for their consideration and assistance, and to J. Byron and K. Byron for checking the scriptural references and for proofreading the manuscript.

Ash Wednesday

In Secret

In the gospel of Matthew (6:1–6, 16–18), Jesus tells his disciples to pray, fast, and give alms "in secret" (en tō kruptō). The root for the word secret is "to hide," especially to hide protectively.

The religion of the bible, perhaps more than any other, insists upon the absolute omniscience and omnipresence of God. It is impossible to hide from God. The psalmist says, "O where can I go from your spirit, or where can I flee from your face? If I climb to the heavens, you are there. If I lie in the grave, you are there" (Ps 139: 7–8). The sinner cannot hide from God. There was no place for Adam and Eve to hide in the Garden of Eden. Still another biblical theme is that the Lord can hide the just protectively under the shadow, the shelter of God's wings, against the violent attacks of the wicked.

Jesus is making a couple of points here. First, God is not interested in the externals; hence, we should not be either. The idea of religion is not that of putting on a good show, however edifying and uplifting it may be. Anybody can see, and misjudge, the externals. However, there is yet another dimension to acting "in secret." What God is interested in is what is in our hearts. And what is in our hearts is hidden from prying eyes, our own included. There are very good reasons why it is inappropriate to judge others' motivations, since we cannot always be certain even of our own. Nevertheless, God does know the secrets of the heart, sometimes because he has put them there, inspirations that motivate us to do what needs doing.

God knows the good we do in secret. And that's all that counts.

Thursday After Ash Wednesday

Crosses

My impression is that most people have heavier crosses to bear than I do. When I listen to the life stories of others, the problems they have, I know I should not complain about some of the minor issues I have to put up with. Which does not mean, of course, that I do not complain.

"Jesus said to all"—to all—"Whoever wishes to be my follower must deny his (or her) very self, take up his (or her) cross each day, and follow in my steps" (Lk 9:23).

When it comes to crosses, we usually do not have to seek them out. They are generally laid upon us: physical ill-health, financial problems of one sort or another, the emotional distress caused by a worrisome loved one.

But there is another and more immediate source for our crosses: ourselves. At times, we make our own crosses. Now you might think that we would have the good sense to make well-upholstered crosses, with nice cushions for carrying them. But it does not normally work that way. The crosses we create for ourselves are often the worst.

In his letter to the Galatians (6:2), St. Paul says that we are to bear one another's burdens and thus fulfill the law of Christ. The opposite of this is precisely what Jesus condemns in the practice of the scribes and Pharisees: "They bind heavy burdens, hard to bear, and lay them on other people's shoulders; but they themselves will not move them with their finger" (Mt 23:4).

Bearing others' burdens sometimes means, I think, taking the crosses people sometimes burden themselves with and dropping them over the nearest cliff. This is the meaning of a number of Jesus' cures. Granted, there may be cases where we are unable to take care of the crosses of others in this way, either because we are not given the opportunity, or because they will not let us do so. For some, crosses are curious things. They can be signs for ourselves, or others, of how much we are suffering. They can be forms of self-punishment. Also, since they are our crosses, we can become personally attached to them. They are our very own personal crosses. We prefer them to some new and unfamiliar one. In such cases, what we can do for others by way of helping them with their burden is to pray that Jesus will lift the cross from their shoulders, and drop it over the nearest cliff.

Friday After Ash Wednesday

Feasting and Fasting

There are parties, and there are parties. There are those to which one is invited, parties that, for one reason or another, one feels obliged to attend. You do not really want to go, so you plan to put in a brief appearance and escape as quickly as possible. There are also parties that should have been good, but which, because of the mix of people, or because you get cornered by the party bore, or say the wrong thing, turn out to be disasters.

In the gospel of Matthew (9:14–15), disciples of John the Baptizer ask Jesus why his disciples do not fast, as the Pharisees fast, as John's disciples fast. Jesus presents the image of a wedding party with himself as the groom. You don't fast at a wedding party. It would be an insult to the groom.

There is another side to the image employed here by Jesus. In the Hebrew context a marriage is a covenant, like the covenant between God and Israel, a covenant that the prophet Hosea, among others, describes as a marriage. So when Jesus likens himself to the groom at a wedding feast, there is the subtle suggestion that with his coming, with his presence, a new covenant is in the offing.

That calls for a celebration. We are invited. We have an engraved invitation from the father of the bridegroom to a party given in his son's honor. It should be a great party. After all, the host had the reputation of being a glutton and a drunkard. Granted, the party may seem to have the wrong mix: the guest list includes tax collectors and sinners. But if you are an acknowledged sinner you should feel right at home. Fast? You can do that later. You have the whole rest of Lent. For now it's a feast. And Jesus is the life of the party.

Saturday After Ash Wednesday

Matthew, the Tax Collector

The general perception of people is that if someone is rich, they probably did something shady or dishonest somewhere along the line to get that way. This was most certainly the perception of tax collectors in Jesus' time. In the gospels, they are invariably coupled with sinners, *hamartoloi.* Matthew (Levi) was a tax collector.

There were several things the Jewish authorities did not like about Jesus the rabbi, the teacher. He performed healings on the Sabbath. Jesus' response: the Sabbath is made for people, not people for the Sabbath. He taught women the law; he had women as his disciples. That is the meaning of the phrase regarding Mary's—of Martha and Mary fame—"sitting at the feet of Jesus." Jesus' response: Mary has chosen the better part and it shall not be taken from her. And he consorted with tax collectors and sinners. Jesus' response: it is not the healthy that need a physician, but the sick.

We are also aware of what Jesus had to say about wealth. Even allowing for Near Eastern hyperbole and exaggeration, Jesus' saying that it is easier for a camel to pass through the eye of a needle than for a rich man to enter the kingdom of heaven is pretty strong stuff. Matthew was a rich man. He could afford to host a dinner for Jesus and a large group of his fellow tax collectors.

Yet, Jesus called Matthew, a rich man, a tax collector, a sinner, to follow him; and he did (Lk 5:27–29). All of a sudden Matthew could become what he could not have been before—free.

The freedom of the sons and daughters of God is an important theme in the letters of St. Paul. It is also part of the meaning of mature adulthood found in the letter to the Ephesians, a maturity that attains the measure of the stature of the fullness of Christ. It is a freedom from sin, a freedom from all those things that can hinder us from becoming what God would have us be. As such, it is more than strictly a human freedom. It is a divine freedom that calls and invites a human response. It is God's own freedom and power to save.

First Sunday of Lent

The Last Temptation

That Jesus should have been tempted at all can appear to some as something of a scandal. After all, if Christ is God and God created all things, then God also created the angel gone bad, the devil or Satan, the one who tempted Jesus. However, Jesus is also fully human, and was tempted just as we are, as the letter to the Hebrews (4:15) reminds us: "For we have not a high priest who is unable to sympathize with our weaknesses, but one who in every respect has been tempted as we are, yet without sinning." Also in Hebrews (2:18): "And because he himself has...been tempted, he is able to help those who are tempted."

It would be a mistake to imagine, as a film some years back did, that Jesus' last temptation was one of lust or regret at not having led a more normal life, taken a wife and had a family. Rather, the last temptation of Christ is on the lips of his enemies, who taunt him from the foot of the cross: "He saved others; let him save himself..." or "If he is the Son of God, let him come down from the cross and we will believe in him." The last temptation of Jesus was to use his divine power to save his human life and, thereby, prove in a definitive way his divine claim. The last temptation of Jesus is the temptation to power.

So were Jesus' first temptations, as they are given in the gospel of the first Sunday of Lent. They are temptations to power: manifest your power by changing stones into bread to feed yourself and a hungry world; manifest your power by taking over the rule of the world to make it a better place; manifest your power by leaping off the top of the temple so that, when God saves you, everyone will know that you are God's anointed.

Our most serious temptations, those with the most serious consequences for others, and for ourselves in the long run, are temptations to exercise control, to exert power over the lives of others, to manipulate others for our own aims and purposes. The predominant drive in the rapist is not sexual. Rather, it is the power he exercises over his victim. Those who abuse children exercise abusive power, quite often, as we know, because abusive power was exercised over them.

On the other hand, if there is one thing we learn about Jesus—and the Christ is a manifestation of God his father—it is that the all-powerful God does not go around flaunting his power in a showy or flashy way. God is, indeed, in control of things. However, he does not control, or take control, of our lives. *We* are supposed to do that. God does not use his power to manipulate us but, rather, to let us grow and go free.

Jesus did not best the devil on the occasion of the temptations in the desert described in today's gospel. The tempter and the temptation would be back again at the very end of Jesus' life: If you are the Son of God, save yourself; come down from the cross and we will believe. Jesus resisted that last temptation. He did not come down from the cross. However, by not doing so, he finally, and totally, overcame the power of Satan. And by that cross, by his passion and death, he wrought our salvation.

Monday of the First Week

Sheep and Goats

"You shall love your neighbor as yourself," says Leviticus (19:18). Leviticus puts the case negatively: You shall not steal, lie, swear falsely, defraud, bear hatred in your heart, take revenge, bear a grudge, and so forth. You would not want to be treated in such a fashion, so do not treat others that way.

Jesus, on the other hand, tells you what you are supposed to be doing positively: You are to feed the hungry, welcome the stranger, visit those who are ill or in prison, and so forth. You would want to be treated in that fashion, so treat others the same way.

There is another difference between the two passages that is a little more subtle. Leviticus says, "You shall love your neighbor as yourself." And why? Because "I am the Lord, your God, and I am holy." The biblical meaning of the word *holy* is something that is separate, set apart. God is totally set apart from all lying, revenge, slander, standing idly by when someone's life is at stake, and so forth. You are to be separate, and separate yourself, from all such actions. You are to be holy as the Lord your God is holy.

In Matthew's gospel (25:31–46), on the other hand, the reason Jesus gives for feeding the hungry, clothing the naked, visiting the sick, in other words, taking care of and caring for those in need, is that what you do to the least one of your brothers or sisters "you do it to me."

In other words, if you take care of the needs of your brother or sister, Jesus takes it personally. And if you do not take care of the needs of your brother or sister, Jesus takes that personally too.

Tuesday of the First Week

Our Father

I have this theory about heaven. We can't get in until we are willing to forgive those who have offended us, and until we ask, and are willing to accept, the forgiveness of others. This is how I understand purgatory—going through the process of forgiving those who have hurt or harmed us. It is also the process of asking and accepting the forgiveness of those we have hurt or harmed. This may sound easy. But just consider what is involved. The murder victim must forgive his or her murderer; the victims of injustice, those who were unjust to them; those who have been abused, their abusers. Forgiveness seldom comes cheap and easy.

Why must we forgive? Because we have been forgiven. And we are forgiven infinitely more than we are asked to forgive. In the Our Father, we pray that we may be forgiven in the measure that we forgive. The Our Father is really a very dangerous prayer to say. For it implies that if we do not forgive those who have offended us, then we cannot expect to be forgiven our offenses.

There is not only forgiving, there is also forgetting. If we follow current events at all we know how true this is. When we look at the former Yugoslavia or the Middle East we see peoples with memories that are far too long. They cannot seem to forget. They remember everything. Sometimes we may say, I can forgive him or her for that, but I will never forget. If we cannot forget we have probably not really forgiven, not totally let it go.

However, there is another side to forgiveness that we sometimes ignore. We are aware of God's forgiveness in our lives, and of the need to forgive others. But there is also God. Sometimes we have to forgive God. This may sound odd. Still, I think it is true. It is possible for us to become angry with God for a particular cross or trial we have to bear, a physical disability, a difficult family situation, a painful illness. Alcoholics or homosexuals can sometimes be quite upset with God for the hand they have been dealt. Forgiveness and asking the forgiveness of others loom larger in our lives than we sometimes realize, and are also a big part of our eternal lives as well. For God has invited us all, all of us, to his heavenly banquet. However, we do not make the seating arrangements. We may be seated next to someone, who is, or was, not exactly our favorite person on earth. But he or she *will* be; otherwise it would not be heaven.

Wednesday of the First Week

Sign of Jonah

The meaning of the Sign of Jonah in the gospel of St. Luke (11:29–32) is not the same as in the gospel of St. Matthew. In Matthew (12:38–42), the Sign of Jonah means that Jesus will be in the bowels of the earth for three days prior to his resurrection, just as Jonah was in the belly of the whale for three days.

The slant Luke gives to the Sign of Jonah emphasizes, rather, the effectiveness and power of Jesus' preaching. It is like the preaching of Jonah, which caused the Gentile Ninevites, the whole people, to repent, and perhaps even included the cattle and sheep, since they also fasted from food and water. In Jesus, God's spokesperson, even greater power is manifest. Luke also holds up the example of the generous response of the Ninevites, who are not the chosen people, to his Gentile readers.

Jesus' Word, the Word of God that Jesus is, is power—power to transform lives, to turn minds and hearts around in repentance. Further, it is the power of those transformed lives to transform the lives of others.

There is only one catch. We have to allow that Word, the power of that Word, which Jesus speaks and is, to effect its work within us, and through us, for others. God's Word can save, if we will but let it.

Thursday of the First Week

Getting It Right

In science, getting the right question, separating out the right sample, setting up the right experiment, is more than half the battle. Indeed, if one does not ask the right question, it is unlikely that one will receive the right answer; if one does not seek the answer to the problem with the right experiment, the solution will not likely be found; if one does not knock on the right door, the entrance to knowledge will not be opened.

Scientists are also aware that they can get the wrong sample, that experiments can fail, and that some of the solutions they come up with may have by-products or side-effects that are not of human benefit. Nuclear energy was a marvelous discovery. What to do with nuclear waste over the long term remains a serious concern.

God is not like science, giving with one hand, taking with another. God is merciful and full of compassion. This does not mean that God gives us everything we ask for. We can, after all, knock on the wrong door, seek salvation in the wrong place, pick the wrong samples of his goodness. However, even when we may ask for the wrong thing, ask for something that is not really good for us, we have to believe that what we will receive is what the God who loves us chooses in his infinite goodness to give.

Friday of the First Week

Settling Out of Court

We live in a litigious society—everybody suing everyone else over just about anything. More lawyers exist per capita in our country than in any other nation in the world. Whether there are more lawyers because there are more lawsuits or more lawsuits because there are more lawyers is difficult to say. In any case, Jesus gives some free legal advice that is still valid: settle out of court (Mt 5:25).

Children often say, whether while playing games, or when a sibling gets a larger piece or portion, "That's not fair." It is only later in life that they may come to agree with the cynical truth that life is not fair. But God is fair, says Ezekiel (18:21–28). However, do not imagine that the meaning of God's fairness is the same as ours; God's ways are not ours. Remember the people who came in at the eleventh hour receiving the same wage as those who had worked all day? Remember the man in the gospel who had one talent, saved it, and then had it taken away?

Is God fair? Well, were we born equal? All equally wealthy, beautiful, handsome, witty, clever? No, we are not born equal, despite what the Declaration of Independence may say. Then again, on second thought, maybe we are. According to biologists, we are all born with half a dozen defective genes. However, in each one of us, they just happen to be *different* defective genes. Or the theologians might remind us that we are all equally born with original sin. This kind of "equality," I am sure, would not have been applauded by the Enlightenment-influenced founders of our country. Well, is that fair? I don't know. It's the human condition, the way things are. Still, one thing is true: whatever the cards dealt us, God expects us to play those cards the best we can. Is that fair? God says it is.

Saturday of the First Week

Loving the Enemy

There are obvious problems with the command to love, if you really think about it. This aside from the even more obvious problems involved with loving one's enemies. For love does not seem to be one of those things that can be activated on command. It is clearly not possible to force another to love us. "Either you love me, or I will beat you up" is not going to work.

Now we may be willing to heed the command to love if we think we are going to get something out of it. Jesus alludes to this when he says, "If you love those who love you, what merit is there in that?" (Mt 5:46). But this also means that if we love someone who hates us, or has done us ill, because we think we are going to get a reward in heaven, then we do not really love that other person—we just love what we're going to get out of fulfilling the command to love. That won't work either.

Or we can take the approach Paul suggests in Romans (12:20, quoting Prv 25:21–22), "…if your enemies are hungry, feed them; if they are thirsty, give them something to drink; for by doing this you will heap burning coals on their heads." In other words, do nice things for your enemies. It will drive them crazy.

Love has to be freely given if it is to be genuine. It has to be from the heart. In the bible, the heart is the seat of physical vitality. It is also the innermost part of our being, the source of thought and reflection, the seat of the will and the origin of our resolves. Feelings, emotions, passions, and desires arise from the heart. Last, but by no means least, religious conduct and moral behavior are rooted in the heart.

It is the heart, and changing the heart, that Jesus is getting at. And changing our hearts, changing the way we feel about someone who has wronged us, someone who persecutes us, requires a superhuman effort. In the final analysis, it requires divine grace. Jesus enjoins us to pray for our persecutors. For there is grace involved in praying for the good of those who persecute us, a grace for them, but also one that will enable us to do what we pray for, that is, love our enemies and those who persecute us.

Second Sunday of Lent

Transfiguration

Some scripture scholars maintain that the transfiguration event is a transposition of a postresurrection appearance back into the earthly life of Jesus. I suppose that could be. I don't know.

Even if so, that does not in any way affect the difficulty the disciples had with Jesus. For, throughout his ministry, Jesus was being transfigured before their eyes. They experienced a divine power flowing through his words and actions, through his teachings and in the healings and cures he performed. Thus, he could easily be seen as associated with Moses, the great lawgiver and teacher, and with Elijah, the great prophet and miracle worker.

Charismatics, holy persons, saints, can have an aura about them. Those halos pictured around the heads of saints are not merely an artist's touch. However, it is not just around the head, but about the whole body. I have no trouble believing that Jesus had such an aura about his person (which may have been more or less intense at one time or another), above all in the presence of his intimate disciples.

The importance of the transfiguration event for his disciples, and for us his disciples, is not simply that it looks forward beyond Jesus' passion and death to his resurrection, but that it looks forward beyond our own individual death to our own resurrection—to a time, or better, to an eternity when we will have our own little aura. Indeed, our lives on earth can be looked upon as the time when we are being measured for our own personal halo.

Monday of the Second Week

Be Compassionate as Your Father Is Compassionate

According to Sigmund Freud, the two principal causes of neuroses are sex and religion—sex because of arrested development, and religion because of the guilt trips that it lays on people.

Jesus expresses some of his objections to the pharisaic view of religion, among them: "They bind heavy burdens, hard to bear, and lay them on men's shoulders; but they themselves will not move them with their finger" (Mt 23:4).

In Jesus' view, they make of religion an intolerable burden. What Jesus is providing, in a way, is a test for religion or, at least, for our understanding of religion. We can ask ourselves the following questions: Does our religion enable us to rise up to God, or is it a dead weight on our backs? Does it make us joyful or cause us to be depressed? Does it carry us, or do we carry it? Indeed, our religion teaches us that we are to bear our burdens and carry our crosses. However, the religion itself is not supposed to be one of those burdens or crosses. Rather, it is supposed to help us carry our burdens, our crosses, with joy.

In other words, if your religion or the view you have of it is only making matters worse, then there is probably something wrong with your view of religion and, perhaps more seriously, with your view of God. For does not Jesus say in the gospel of Matthew (11:29), "Take my yoke upon you, and learn from me; for I am gentle and lowly in heart, and you will find rest for your souls"?

That is what your religion is supposed to be doing for you. We'll talk about sex some other time.

Tuesday of the Second Week

Religious Institutions

Solomon has built a temple. Building a temple for God is religion; the temple is religion. Yet, Solomon recognizes that this temple does not and cannot contain the God for whom it is built and to whom it is dedicated: "Behold, heaven and the highest heaven cannot contain thee; how much less this house which I have built!" (1 Kgs 8:27). Religion is meant to address the interests of God; it does not contain God. For God, at times, sends his prophets to preach repentance to the religion itself.

Jesus, who is himself one of those prophets, makes something of the same point. Ritual washings or religious observances can be part of the traditions of a religion. However, Jesus notes that religious traditions can, at times, operate against true religion. Jesus insists that a religion is meant to address the interests of God; it cannot, any more than the temple, contain God. To imagine that God can somehow be trapped within some particular religious tradition or institutional form or set of external practices is to misunderstand the nature of religion and, in the final analysis, the nature of God. For it fails to understand God's universal power to save. And it fails to understand the obligation of religion, any religion, to proclaim that universal power to save and to be open to the prophetic voices that remind the religion of this truth.

Wednesday of the Second Week

Service

According to present-day economists, the U.S. economy is primarily service-oriented. This is especially the case if we include all those working for the government. For the majority of Americans are involved, in one way or another, in service areas: professionals, whether doctors or nurses (health services), lawyers or beauticians, civil servants or soldiers, teachers or restaurateurs, and so forth.

There are certain maxims of service, such as "The customer is always right," "Service with a smile," "Garnish is a must." In performing a service, one is expected to fulfill it dutifully, on time and in time, with ease, and without a lot of muss and fuss. We expect any service to be professionally and competently performed.

Well, we are service men and women, servants of the most high God and, if we want to rank first among our fellow Christians, servants of our fellow brothers and sisters. God and his servants are the customers; and the customer is always right. We are expected to fulfill our turn of service dutifully. Further, it is supposed to be service with a smile; garnish is a must. And finally, the service is to be on time and in time, performed with ease, and without a lot of muss and fuss.

Thursday of the Second Week

Lazarus and Dives

According to the prophet Jeremiah, God describes himself as a searcher of minds and hearts: "I the Lord search the mind and try (or test) the heart" (Jer 17:10).

That God can and does read our hearts can be a consoling thought. He would know that our intentions were good, that we really tried, that we meant well. On the other hand, it may be a less-than-consoling thought to know that the searcher of minds and hearts also sees our pettiness, our less-than-noble motives, our sometimes venal and unkind thoughts.

Jeremiah adds: God rewards everyone according to his or her ways, according to the merit of his or her deeds—for example, the rich man and Lazarus in Luke's gospel (Lk 16:19–31). Why was the rich man judged so harshly? He did not mistreat Lazarus, kick him off his doorstep. He even let his dogs lick Lazarus' sores, though I'm not sure whether this was good or bad. Also, it was not as if the rich man was totally unaware of the poor man's existence. After all, he knew his name: "Father Abraham…send Lazarus to dip the end of his finger in water to cool my tongue…"

It is interesting to note, on the other hand, that the rich man does not have a name; he is just "a rich man," a dime a dozen. The rich man's sin was not what he did to the poor man. Indeed, he let him beg at the gate of his house. The rich man's sin lay in his attitude. As George Bernard Shaw put it, "The worst sin in the world is not to hate our fellow human beings but to be indifferent toward them." The rich man recognized the existence of the poor man, but dealt with him as though he did not exist.

It's not what he did, but what he did not do. He just didn't care.

Friday of the Second Week

Cornerstone

"You are God's field; you are God's building," Paul says to the Corinthians (1 Cor 3:9).

Because of the nature of the soil in Palestine, which is stony, with outcroppings of limestone, when a farmer clears a field he has to do something with the stones. So he constructs a building with them, or a wall to enclose his field.

In the gospel of Matthew (21:33–43, 45–46), Jesus likens God to a property owner who clears the ground of stones, plants a vineyard, excavates a vat, and uses the stones to build a tower and wall around the vineyard. He then leases the vineyard to tenant farmers. When he sends servants to collect his share of the harvest, they are treated badly or are killed. So the owner decides to send his son, thinking that the tenants will show some respect toward his son. But these evil men, seeing an opportunity to seize the vineyard for themselves, drag him outside the walls and kill him.

Jesus then invites his auditors to consider the owner's response to such wickedness. They draw the correct conclusion. However, Matthew adds a citation from Psalm 118, "The stone the builders rejected has become the cornerstone." The one the wicked tenant farmers thought they had gotten rid of becomes the basis for a new building.

There is an old theological adage that goes back at least to St. Augustine: *Gratia praesupponit natura*, grace builds upon nature. Some things have to be cleared away from our lives if the kingdom of God is to be established in our hearts. But we do not discard those human things. We save the stones. We allow the Spirit of Jesus to divinize our stony hearts by his grace. Hence, I have often thought of turning Augustine's adage around: *Natura praesupponit gratia*, nature builds upon grace. Without the cornerstone, the building will not happen.

Saturday of the Second Week

The Prodigal

In large public or private concerns, businesses, or institutions there is a lost-and-found department. If we find something someone seems to have lost that's where we take it. If we think we have left our umbrella somewhere in the building, we go to the lost and found to see if someone may have turned it in, that is, after we have retraced our steps (and prayed to St. Anthony).

In the parable of the prodigal son (Lk 15:1–3, 11–32), the younger son was lost. When you are lost in the wilderness, it doesn't do any good just to start walking. Chances are that you will just wander around in circles. You have to figure out where you are, then which direction to head in order to get unlost. It had taken time, but finally the prodigal son knew he was lost. He was not where a Jew, even a nonpracticing Jew, wanted to be: among the swine. So he figured out how to get himself unlost. He would swallow his pride, admit he was wrong, and return to his father's house.

Lo and behold, the prodigal son discovered that he had an even more prodigal father. Not only was his father patiently waiting for him to find himself, not only did he not burden him with a guilt-ridden "I told you so," but he dressed his son in finery and had a party thrown in his honor. He had been found. He was alive.

This is much better than being dead and lost.

Third Sunday of Lent

The Stranger

The way Jesus related to women, as especially presented in the gospels of Luke and John, might best be described as casual, proper but casual. This in itself was somewhat odd for a male in the world of ancient Greece, or Rome, or Palestine.

Thus, in John's gospel (4:5–42), it was a bit unusual for Jesus to request a drink of water from the woman at the well. It was also unusual because she was a Samaritan woman. And a Jew would avoid even talking to a Samaritan, let alone accepting something he or she touched. I have often thought what a rude awakening it was for the Jew who fell among robbers to wake up and find that a Samaritan had brought him back to life and was paying his bill at the inn.

There is a problem with the *xeno*, the stranger. The stranger is the foreigner, someone from another place, someone hard to fathom, unsettling, even threatening. Hence our word *xeno-phobia.* Indeed, the underlying sense of the word is enemy. Because no one appreciated being an alien in a foreign land, in the ancient world hospitality, *philoxenia* (love for the stranger or alien), became an iron-clad law. This was true of ancient Greece, for example. In the *Odyssey,* Homer says that those who fear the gods will be gracious to strangers. It was true also in the world of the bible. Deuteronomy says that God loves the stranger (10:19), and so should his people.

We must not imagine that we are immune from negative feelings toward strangers, those who differ from us, those we find disturbing or threatening because they are of another race, a different social class, religion, or sexual orientation. We must always return to the example of Jesus, who was accepting of everyone, including the Samaritan woman at the well.

We must remember that to this woman Jesus was also a stranger. However, both benefited from their encounter. Jesus received a drink of water, and the woman the offer of living water. When strangers accept each other the barriers of hostility come down, to the benefit of both.

Chapter 53 of the *Rule of Benedict* states, "All guests who present themselves are to be welcomed as Christ." In the case of the woman at the well, this was literally true.

Monday of the Third Week

Reminders

There are some things we do not necessarily like to be reminded of, even if they are true, sometimes *especially* if they are true. One may suspect that Jesus did not particularly like being reminded that he was a Nazarene—"Can anything good come out of Nazareth?" asks Nathaniel (Jn 1:46). Especially when he found no acceptance among his own people. One may also suspect that Naaman, the victorious general of Aram, did not appreciate the constant physical reminder of his condition of leprosy (2 Kgs 5:1–15). And it is clear that Jesus' fellow Jews did not like being reminded that God sent his prophets, Elijah and Elisha, to minister not only to Gentiles, the widow of Zarephath, but even to heal one of the enemies of Israel, Naaman the Syrian (Lk 4:24–30).

God is not supposed to act like that. And so, when Jesus reminds his fellow townspeople that God does, indeed, act that way, they react as their ancestors had toward the prophets of old, threatening to destroy Jesus. If we don't like the message, we get rid of the messenger who delivers it. There are reasons why the prophet receives the prophet's reward. If we don't like being reminded of something we reject the one who reminds us.

As we know, that is seldom the end of the matter. There are limits to denial. Naaman remained a leper until he eventually followed Elisha's directions. The prophets sent to the chosen people to remind them of the covenant may have been slain, but God could always raise up another prophet.

It is comforting to know that God does not accept rejection but continually sends reminders.

Tuesday of the Third Week

Forgiveness

In the gospel of Matthew (18:21–35), the king's servant owes his master a truly regal sum. An ordinary day laborer would have to work some 15 years to earn just one talent. And this king's servant owes 10,000 talents! To get that kind of money, the servant would have to be in the drug trade or, in those days, the silk trade. So when the servant throws himself upon the mercy of his master, saying that he will pay everything back, the king knows how empty the promise is. Yet, he forgives his servant the debt.

The servant's fellow servant owes, by comparison, a paltry sum. But the servant whose debt was forgiven is not as merciful as his master in forgiving the debt owed to him. You know the rest of the story. The unforgiving servant gets his old unpayable debt back, with interest.

When we do a favor for someone we may say, or imply, "You owe me." And every once in a while we may be tempted to call in those debts. However, the parable is not just about forgiveness—forgiving others because God has forgiven us so much—it is also about generosity. God does not keep score of the favors he does for us. Hence, neither should we keep score of the favors we do for others.

When we are generous toward another it might be better to say to God, "Just put it on my tab," realizing that it will require doing a lot of favors for a lot of people before we will ever make even the slightest dent in paying off our tab.

Wednesday of the Third Week

The Law and the Prophets

In Matthew's gospel it says: "Think not that I have come to abolish the law and the prophets; I have come not to abolish them but to fulfill them" (5:17). Indeed, from all we can tell Jesus observed the prescriptions of the Torah, while at the same time departing decisively from the pharisaic traditions and interpretations regarding the Torah.

On the other hand, if one were to listen to Paul: "...now we are discharged from the law...so that we serve not under the old written code but in the new life of the Spirit" (Rom 7:6).

According to Matthew, the law is not abolished; according to Paul, it is. Are these two really in the same church? Of course, we could say that they are speaking at two different periods in the church's history, two different stages in the development of early Christianity. But would we not then expect a distancing from Judaism to occur in Matthew, who is later, rather than in Paul, who is earlier?

Now I know of no present-day Christian community that observes all 613 precepts of the Mosaic Law. So from this one might conclude that in the argument between Paul and Matthew, Paul won. Though it is interesting to note that when moral or ethical problems arise in the early Christian communities Paul serviced, more often than not he reverts back to his rabbinical training for solutions.

Nevertheless, if we really wish to understand Matthew's position we need to read further in his gospel. When one of the Pharisees asks Jesus about the great commandment of the law (22:36), his answer is: Love God, and your neighbor as yourself. "On these two commandments depend all the law and the prophets." Paul would most certainly agree that we are not discharged from that law; for this is precisely what he means by life in Christ, life of the Spirit.

The lesson here is that there can be and are serious differences of theological opinion within the church. However, there are also certain basics upon which we remain united.

As Christians, we would say that the law is ordained toward justice; however, it is also our belief that Jesus brings a higher justice, above all, the religious ideal of love. Matthew says this when he speaks of Jesus as the fulfillment of the law, the fulfillment of the law of love. Paul says the same thing when he speaks of new life in the Spirit.

For both, the Christian is to be the fulfillment of that law of love.

Thursday of the Third Week

The Sin Against the Holy Spirit

Jesus' enemies say that it is by the power of the devil that he casts out demons (Lk 11:15). Jesus has little trouble refuting the charge: a kingdom divided against itself will not last. Still, it is a nasty thing to say, accusing someone doing good, casting out evil spirits, of being evil, doing so because he is in league with the devil.

In Chapter 12 of his first letter to the Corinthians, Paul alludes to the importance of the discernment of spirits. We must pray to the Holy Spirit for the gifts of the Spirit so that we may be able to discern the spirits in persons and events to see if they are of God. The need for such guidance is no less important in our so-called enlightened age. Remember that guy some years back, in Guyana, who had his followers drink purple Kool-Aid, or the Davidians in Waco, Texas, or that French-Canadian in Switzerland and the burned chalets with the bodies inside? The difficulty in spotting the religious phonies from the genuine article still exists.

It was obviously no less so for Jesus' contemporaries. So where did the scribes and Pharisees, eminently religious types, go wrong and thereby totally miss the reign of God? One might say that they were just not open to the Spirit. However, it was more serious than that. In the gospels, they are accused of actually blaspheming the Holy Spirit. I suppose one would have to say that among certain religious types—and the more religious they are the more likely this can be an issue—one can get a combination of self-certainty and arrogance that is absolutely deadly from a religious point of view. Well, if we are on God's side and God is on our side, then whatever we condemn must be what God would condemn.

So we do, and we're dead wrong. And the whole business rises like a stench right up to the throne of God.

Friday of the Third Week

The Two Commandments

What Jesus says in response to the question posed by the scribe concerning the basic commandment of the law is not particularly new or original (Mk 12:28–34).

Jesus simply quotes the "Schema O Israel" of Deuteronomy 6:4–9: "Hear, O Israel: The Lord is our God, the Lord alone. You shall love the Lord your God with all your heart, and with all your soul, and with all your might." The text would have been pronounced twice daily by any pious Jew. The second commandment Jesus adds may be found in Leviticus 19:18: You shall love your neighbor as yourself. In other words, Jesus quotes the Torah in a thoroughly traditional fashion.

Further, there is no attempt on Jesus' part somehow to equate the two commandments: we worship God, but no matter how much we may show respect and honor toward our neighbor, we do not worship him or her. Now it's true that in France a lover may say to his beloved *Je t'adore,* I adore thee. However, as far as I am aware, not even in France does this imply getting down on one's knees and bowing one's forehead to the floor.

What is unique in Jesus' teaching is the juxtaposing of the two commandments, each of which contains the word *love.* When those two commandments are set right next to each other in our lives, then, as Jesus tells the insightful scribe, we are not far from the kingdom of God. For then we live in God's love and that love overflows from us into the lives of others. On the other hand, the converse is equally true: if the two commandments are set apart from each other, if we do not worship God in spirit and in truth and treat others as we would have them treat us, then, by the same token, we remove ourselves far from the kingdom of God.

Saturday of the Third Week

The Pharisee and the Publican

In Hindi, one of the languages of India, the word for bribe is *sandosh,* which means "something that makes someone else happy." The word has a root in Sanskrit, the language of ancient India, which indicates that bribery has been a way of doing business in the Indian culture for a very long time. The Pharisee in today's gospel (Lk 18:9–14) attempts what might be called religious bribery. He thanks God for all the religiously incorrect things he is not and does not do, and he points out to God all the right things that he is and does. In effect, the Pharisee is saying: God, you owe me. The Pharisee had not taken to heart that line from Sirach (35:11): "Do not offer him a bribe, for he will not accept it...." It is impossible to bribe God, no matter how goody-goody we may think we are.

The parable about the Pharisee and the tax collector plays upon three themes: the righteous, the unrighteous, and the self-righteous. However, Jesus upsets the standard reading of the categories. The person who appears to be righteous is not justified; the one who appears to be unrighteous is justified through the recognition of his need for God's mercy. And the Pharisee? Well, the self-righteous person has no need of God's justification, since he has justified himself, which means that he is not really justified at all. So much for the Pharisee.

Now back to the tax collector; he has nothing with which to bribe God. On the contrary, he's on the wrong side of everything: the religious law, his own society, his own self-respect. He is thoroughly despised by his fellow Jews because he collects taxes for the hated Romans. He is, at best, a collaborator, at worst, a traitor. Further, there is a bad odor attached to his line of work, the suspicion that he overcollects and pockets the difference.

So what should he do? Well, you might say, all he has to do

is quit collecting taxes. Wait a minute. Then what does he do? How does he support himself? One can readily imagine him saying what the unjust steward said in another of Jesus' parables: "To dig I am not able, to beg I am ashamed" (Lk 16:3). Let us say he actually quits his line of work. His fellow Jews will still hate him for what he was. He is trapped, stuck.

The tax collector is not the first person to be trapped in a situation from which he can see no way out. Nor will he likely be the last. How about someone who is in a marriage not recognized by the church? Is he or she supposed to leave the spouse and abandon the children? There is only the tax collector's prayer: "Have mercy on me, O God, a sinner." How about people with a serious drug problem? They try to break out of the cycle, and keep falling back into it. There is only the tax collector's prayer: "Have mercy on me, O God, a sinner." Or how about people in a state of enmity toward each other, a relative with whom we have been at odds for years. At this juncture, we may be unable to think of a way of even starting to make peace. There is only the tax collector's prayer: "Have mercy on me, O God, a sinner."

In other words, when you have absolutely nothing with which to bribe God—and you really don't—you say the tax collector's prayer.

A final note: this plea will not necessarily work with the Internal Revenue Service.

Fourth Sunday of Lent

Eternal Life Now

In the gospel of St. John, everything important is in the present tense. Jesus says, "Very truly, I tell you, anyone who hears (present tense) my word and believes (present tense) him who sent me has (present tense) eternal life, and does not come (present tense) under judgment..." (5:24). If we hear, heed, and take in the words that Jesus speaks, make them part of ourselves, part of our lives, then we live, here and now, the eternal life of God.

For who is it that sent that word of God, the Word of God that is Jesus, into the world but the one whom Jesus calls Abba, Father?

According to Freud, God is a father-image, a stern (Germanic?) patriarchal figure who, like an angry father, punishes us when we violate the commandments thundered down from Mt. Sinai. But although Freud's background was Jewish, one may wonder whether he ever read that beautiful passage from Isaiah (49:15): "Can a woman forget her nursing child, or show no compassion for the child of her womb? Even these may forget, yet I will not forget you." In light of this passage, it would seem that Freud might have done better to speak of God as a mother-image rather than a father-image, or at least a father with a mother's love and tenderness. One of the medieval mystics—I think it is Julian of Norwich—refers to Jesus as mother. Well, after all, if Jesus is life-giver, then Jesus is also mother.

Still, there is a judgment and a condemnation, and each is also in the present tense. However, it is a judgment one brings upon oneself, a condemnation wherein one is self-condemned. In the parable of the talents, there was the servant who received the single talent, buried it, and later restored it to his master, saying, "I knew you were a harsh man, reaping where you did not sow..." (Lk 19:21), and so forth. The servant stands self-condemned. What Jesus is saying in the parable is if that is how you view God, then that is precisely how God will treat you.

In other words, one may, if one wishes, take Freud's view of God as a stern Germanic father, or the servant's "hard master" in Jesus' parable, or that of the Puritan divine Jonathan Edwards—"sinners in the hands of an angry God." However, it strikes me that the view of God as solicitous mother is both more appealing and closer to the truth of an eternal life that we have, that we live, even here and now.

Monday of the Fourth Week

Hospitality

The story of Jesus healing the servant of the centurion at Capernaum is found in three different gospel traditions (Mt 8:5–13, Lk 7:1–10, Jn 4:46–54). The centurion or royal official was probably not a Roman. More than likely he was head of a troop of soldiers in the service of Herod Antipas. He was a Gentile, however, not a Jew. The one healed could have been the centurion's son rather than his servant. The Greek word *pais* can mean either; so can, apparently, the Aramaic word. Jesus heals the son or servant at a distance. He is amazed at, emotionally moved, even edified, by the centurion's faith. In St. John's version of the story the emotional angle is left out. The Johannine tradition tends to emphasize Jesus' divinity more than his humanity.

Not that there is anything wrong with human emotions. Jesus had them and manifested them. Speaking of human emotions, I have always enjoyed that reading from Genesis (18:12–15), Sarah's laughing over the idea that she would have a child in her old age, then trying to say she didn't laugh. "Oh yes, you did," says the Lord.

One of the points of the Genesis story is that hospitality has its reward. Abraham shows hospitality toward his three guests, who turn out to be the one Lord, and is promised an offspring. In Matthew's version of the healing of the centurion's servant, or son, the centurion protests his unworthiness, as a Gentile, even to have Jesus accept his hospitality. We hear what Jesus says about those who believe and have faith in what he is able to do. Many, including Gentiles such as the centurion, will come from east and west and will eat with Abraham and Isaac and Jacob in the kingdom of heaven. God returned the hospitality of Abraham. Not only did God give him a son, but numerous offspring, among whom we also are numbered.

God is always the perfect host. He will make a return to us on whatever hospitality we show to him in the persons of his sons and daughters.

Tuesday of the Fourth Week

Sheep Pool

I recall being in Jerusalem, the Holy City, the holy city for three religions. I was there during Ramadan, and in the evening ate at a small restaurant in the Arab section. There were not many patrons, but there would be after the sun went down, and the Muslims went off their fast. I was also there on a Sabbath, walking through one of the Jewish sections. It was very quiet, no sign of any activity. Even the dogs and cats seemed to move about quietly. For pious Jews the Sabbath is still special, as it was in the days of Jesus.

In his time, Jesus had a reputation as a healer. So when he healed the man at the Sheep Pool (Bethesda) and told him to pick up his mat and walk, some of the man's fellow Jews saw in this a violation of the Sabbath rest and questioned the man about it (Jn 5:1–3, 5–16). He later found out that Jesus was the one who had told him to do this, and he informed on Jesus to the authorities. I suppose it's not the first time in the history of the world that someone performed a good action and got in trouble for it. Fearing a malpractice suit, a doctor may hesitate to treat someone ill on the street or at the roadside, under less than ideal conditions.

Jesus did not go out of his way to perform miraculous cures, certainly not the flashy ones that might attract a great deal of attention. On the contrary, by all accounts he tried to keep the healings he performed quiet and private, between himself and the particular person. He dealt with people personally. Indeed, that is the way we should deal with those who may need our ministrations, our care and concern—quietly, privately, and in a personal way.

Wednesday of the Fourth Week

Scattering and Gathering

If you dust or dust-mop a room in your house you are going to raise dust. Now I am not saying this to discourage anyone from dusting or dust-mopping. I do it myself, once a week, whether it needs it or not. It usually does. Still, when you enter a situation, above all if you enter it forcefully, you disturb and, to some extent, alter the situation. Cultural anthropologists are familiar with the phenomenon. When they bring their tape recorders and cameras into a primitive society to study it, their very presence alters the culture they study. It is now less primitive than it was before their arrival. When Saul and other zealous Jews proceeded against the heretical sect of Christianity the same thing occurred. As the Acts of the Apostles says, "Now those who were scattered went about preaching the word"(8:4). By attacking the early Christian community at its center, Saul and his associates only caused it to spread further abroad.

In the gospel of John, on the other hand, Jesus says, "All that the Father gives me will come to me…" (6:37). Jesus does not scatter or disperse; he gathers together. He speaks even of the ingathering of the dead: An hour is coming when all those in the tombs will hear the voice of God's Son and come forth (Jn 5:28–29). It is interesting that the word for church in the New Testament, *ekklesia,* means, literally, those who are called, gathered, and assembled together to hear God's Word, to be with the Word that is God.

Our lives are often dispersed by the tasks we are called upon to perform. Thus, it is always well to recall where our center is, the center to which, or better, to whom we must always return, namely Christ, the center of our lives of faith, of hope, and of love.

Thursday of the Fourth Week

Covenants

Once in a while, God would become quite upset with the chosen people because of their infidelity to the covenant. On one occasion (Ex 32:7–14), when God threatens them with destruction, Moses tries to shame God into relenting: What will the Egyptians say? You freed them from Egypt only to bring them out into the wilderness, and then slay them? And he uses an argument that many a present-day debtor-nation uses: You've already invested so much in these people that to write them off as a bad debt now would mean losing your whole investment. Fortunately for the chosen people, Moses' argument, based on God's self-interest, prevailed.

Jesus also sometimes loses patience with his contemporaries. He reproaches the chosen people, especially its leaders (Jn 5:31–47): "You search the scriptures, because you think that in them you have eternal life; but it is they that bear witness to me...." They appeal to Moses, and Jesus appeals to Moses. However, Jesus insists that Moses would be on his side, not theirs: If you believed Moses, says Jesus, you would believe me, for he wrote of me. After all, Moses wrote the law, and the Jesus of John's gospel represents the fulfillment of that covenant law.

Covenant law implies obligations of fidelity on both sides. So there is nothing wrong, every now and then, with reminding God, as Moses does, of the investment he has already made in us, and that if he wants to see any of that investment back it is in his best interest to help us when we are in need or distress.

Besides—and this is the clincher—think what people will say if you don't.

Friday of the Fourth Week

Messiah

When Jesus asked the question, "Who do people say that I am?" (Mk 8:27), it was not as though he were suffering from an identity crisis, quite unsure of who he really was. Nor would it necessarily be correct to say that Jesus was an extrovert, that the way he processed information was by bouncing ideas or questions off of other people, in this case his disciples.

People who know where they came from, their origins, and where they are going, know who they are. Jesus knew his origins (Jn 7:28–29), not Nazareth in Galilee, but, rather, the origins of the power he manifested in his ministry of teaching and healing. It came from God. Jesus also knew his destination. Anyone who is aware not only that he is going to die, but knows *how* he is going to die, and accepts the fact and manner of that death, knows who he is. Jesus knew what awaited him: "...the Son of man must suffer many things, and be rejected by the elders and the chief priests and the scribes and be killed, and after three days rise again" (Mk 8:31). And the author of the gospel adds: "And he said this plainly." Jesus clearly knew what was ahead of him.

Jesus also knew that he was doing the will of the one who sent him, the one he called his father. He was to bring peace, which in the biblical context means reconciliation. This was more than simply the dove flying back to the ark with the olive branch in its beak, symbolizing peace between the rainy heavens and a flooded earth (Gn 8:11). Jesus is more than merely a symbol of peace. By hanging on a cross between heaven and earth, Jesus is himself the reconciliation between a sinful humanity and a holy God.

Saturday of the Fourth Week

Lost Anyway

John the Baptizer, from prison, sent two of his disciples to Jesus to inquire: "Are you the one who is to come, or are we to wait for another?" (Lk 7:20). Jesus sent back the response, "Go and tell John what you have seen and heard: the blind receive their sight, the lame walk, the lepers are cleansed, the deaf hear, the dead are raised, the poor have the good news brought to them" (Lk 7:22). Jesus preached the good news to the poor.

The poor were not just those without property or without means, the destitute. Essentially they were God's poor, the *anawim*, the powerless, those whose only hope was in a gracious God. However, the *anawim* could also include the rich (for example, tax collectors), those excluded and despised by the official Judaism of the period.

Jesus' attitude toward such religious outcasts was in sharp contrast with the view of the religious authorities of the time. Jesus ate with tax collectors and sinners, shared table fellowship with them. The attitude of Jewish officialdom, on the other hand, was: "But this crowd, which does not know the law—they are lost anyway" (Jn 7:49). One is reminded of the way the Pharisee looked down upon the tax collector in Luke's gospel: "I thank you, God, that I am not like...this tax collector" (Lk 18:11).

What is the good news Jesus preaches to God's poor? Theirs is the kingdom of heaven (Lk 6:20). It is as though Jesus were saying, fortunate *(makarios)* are the unfortunate. The kingdom of God represents a complete reversal of the established order. Through the good news that Jesus heralds, the poor and the outcasts receive entrance into God's kingdom, a kingdom in which those who mourn shall be comforted, a kingdom in which the hungry, above all those who hunger for justice and holiness, will have their fondest dreams realized.

Hopefully, that is where we are.

Fifth Sunday of Lent

The Johannine Jesus

There are times when one may gain the impression that the Johannine Jesus' feet barely touch the ground. He seems to be totally in control of his human destiny; he seems to just walk away from dangers or threats to his person; he walks on water toward his terrified disciples in the boat on the lake; he is in constant communion with his Father, as though he were in heaven on earth; and even when his time has come, it is a time that he sets.

However, this apparent loftiness is only a semblance. The Jesus of John's gospel is a Jesus who is lifted up from the earth, which indicates that it was on the earth that his feet were placed. And the Johannine Jesus is a person with emotions, indeed deep emotions. After the death of Lazarus when Mary came to meet Jesus, she and all those with her were weeping, and John's gospel says that Jesus was "troubled in spirit, moved by the deepest emotions" (11:33). On the way to the tomb it says that Jesus began to weep, that he was troubled in spirit as he approached the tomb, causing those who were with Martha and Mary to remark, "See, how much he loved him!" (11:36).

The feet of the Johannine Jesus may only lightly touch the earth, but his heart is very much with those who inhabit the earth, above all with his friends, in their love and in their grief.

Jesus called Lazarus forth from the tomb. However, Lazarus would die again, and Jesus would not be around the next time to resuscitate his friend back to earthly life. Having himself risen from the grave, however, Jesus would be in a position to raise his friend Lazarus, as well as us, in the resurrection unto an entirely new life in which there will be no more dying or grieving, forever.

Monday of the Fifth Week

Witnesses

Jewish law required two witnesses in any trial. Remember the two wicked judges and Suzanna (Dn 13), or the two false witnesses who came forward at Jesus' trial (Mt 26:60–61)? Also, the witnesses had to give their testimony in the presence of the accused so that he or she could respond to the charges.

If Jewish law required two witnesses for something to be valid or authenticated, the first letter of John says that Jesus had three: the Spirit, the water, and the blood (1 Jn 5:7–8). There is the Spirit: "You are my beloved Son. On you my favor rests" (Mk 1:11). There is the water: Jesus received John's baptism; Jesus himself baptized. And there is the blood: Jesus' ultimate witnessing *(martyria)* to the kingdom, martyrdom.

After Jesus' death, according to John's gospel, one of the soldiers plunged a spear into Jesus' side and there came forth blood and water (19:34). And the Spirit? Jesus had already bowed his head and given up the Spirit (Jn 19:30). But it would be back.

We have been washed in the waters of baptism. We have received Jesus' baptism, baptized with him unto his death. In this we also participate in his martyrdom, thereby witnessing to the presence of the kingdom in our lives. And we have received the Spirit, whereby we are inspired and strengthened to witness to the new life, the eternal life, we have received, and live, in Christ Jesus. Even now, in this life, with all its trials and troubles, its pains and joys, we possess, we live, life in the Spirit.

Tuesday of the Fifth Week

If I Be Lifted Up

The snake is an ambiguous symbol in the bible. After all, it was a serpent that talked Eve and Adam into eating the forbidden fruit in the garden of paradise. This was the bad snake.

On the other hand, in Chapter 21 of the Book of Numbers, those bitten by the fiery serpents had only to look upon the bronze serpent set atop the pole, and they would be cured. This was the good snake.

In Chapter 12 of the gospel of John, the manner and meaning of Jesus' death is given the same symbolism. Jesus says that when he is lifted up on high, on the pole of the cross, he will draw all people to him. Then all will know that he, the one who comes from the Father, the one who is the very revelation of the Father and of the Father's love, will bring about their healing. In other words, in the same way that the bronze serpent was set on the pole so that all who looked upon it would be cured, so all who look upon Jesus lifted up on the cross will see in him the source of their salvation, and will be healed from sin.

The bronze serpent is hair-of-the-dog treatment. Bitten by the fiery serpents, those Israelites who had spoken against the Lord and Moses had but to look upon the bronze image of the serpent and they were healed. Jesus on the cross also represents hair-of-the-dog treatment. Certainly, this is the case if we take seriously the strong language of St. Paul's second letter to the Corinthians (5:21): "For our sake God made him to be sin who knew no sin, so that in him we might become the righteousness of God." Jesus took our sins upon himself, he became sin, so that by his death we might be healed and saved. This is why we look upon and venerate the cross, especially during Passiontide.

In so many ways we have lost the meaning of the symbolic in our culture. We have become all too literal: Just give me the facts. Cut the metaphor. Our lives and our religious imaginations are the poorer as a result. We have to get back to our basic Christian symbols: water, oil, light, beeswax, bread and wine. There is, perhaps, no better time to do this than during the Easter Vigil when we get in touch with the basic elements: the earth, the air, the fire, and the water, the cool air of a spring night, the burning Easter fire, the blessing of the water and the baptism of the catechumens, and the earth that is beginning to come alive again.

And there we are again, back to the basics of our lives and of our faith.

Wednesday of the Fifth Week

Descendants of Abraham

In all four gospels, Jesus is accused by his enemies of harboring a demon or of being in league with the devil.

In the Synoptic gospels (Mk 3:22–30, Mt 12:24–32, Lk 11:15–22), Jesus' defense is that a kingdom divided against itself will not stand. Thus, if he is casting out demons by the power of Beelzebul, Satan's kingdom is in deep trouble.

It was a dreadful charge. So dreadful, indeed, that Matthew characterizes it as blasphemy against the Spirit, as the unforgivable sin.

In the gospel of John (8:40–41), Jesus points out that his enemies are doing what psychologists would call projecting. They accuse him of having a demon whereas, in fact, it is *they* who are under demonic influence, since they seek to kill him, and are thus in league with the one who, from the beginning, is a liar and a murderer.

The argument between Jesus and his enemies is about Abraham. The Jews insist that Abraham is their father. Jesus maintains that he is the equal of Abraham, since he claims the God of Abraham as his father. In other words, the father Jesus claims as his own, and for his followers, is not simply Abraham but Abraham's God.

Chiseled into a band of stone atop the old library building at the University of Freiburg is the sentence, *"Die Wahrheit wird euch frei machen."* (The truth shall make you free.) The implication seems to be that if you spent sufficient time studying in the library or at the university you would become a free person. Anyone involved in education has to believe that there is at least some truth to this, since to be free of the dull weight of ignorance can only be a move in the right direction.

The truth that Jesus proclaims, however, has little to do

with academic freedom or with the truths of science. Rather, what his teaching has to do with is the Truth (with a capital "T"). And Truth according to the gospel of John is simply salvation. To know this Truth is to be free, not simply as a child of Abraham, but, above all, as a child of God.

Thursday of the Fifth Week

Our Father Abraham

By solemn covenant, God promises to Abraham that he (Abraham) will be the father of many nations, that from Abraham's loins kings will spring, that Abraham and his descendants will have the land of Canaan as an everlasting possession, and, most important, God promises Abraham that he (God) will be his descendants' God (Gn 17:3-9).

Jesus says that Abraham would have rejoiced to see his (Jesus') day (Jn 8:56). Why? Because Jesus represents the fulfillment of those promises given by God to Abraham. Jesus will sit upon the throne of David his father, and he will reign as king forever. Finally, from Jesus will spring a royal people who will be part of an everlasting kingdom; since, as the gospel says, those who keep his word will never taste death (Jn 8:51).

We are the sons and daughters of that ancient covenant made between God and Abraham, renewed in Jesus Christ. It is not a covenant in the flesh, as is the case with the Jews and the descendants of Ishmael, but a covenant in the spirit. Still, as with the Jews and the Arabs, we can claim Abraham as our father, our father in faith.

Let us rejoice in the promise given to our father Abraham, and in the fulfillment of that promise in Christ Jesus our Lord.

Friday of the Fifth Week

Blasphemy

Some real problems exist with a standing army. As long as there is an enemy to fight, a campaign to be planned and executed, the army is at one, united against the common foe. An army in peacetime is another matter entirely. Without an enemy to attack or to defend against, its aggressive instincts are often turned toward its own members, particularly the weaker or more vulnerable.

This was true of the Jews who went after Jesus for blasphemy. Jesus' response was simple enough: Even if you put no faith in my works, put faith in the Father's work that I perform (Jn 10:38).

The same sort of internal persecution can occur within the church militant. The gospel of John presumes that hostility from an unbelieving world will be a permanent feature in the life of Christians. Indeed, when the church is persecuted the members band together, put aside their differences, hunker down, and do their best to ride out the storm. Unfortunately, when the church is not being persecuted, it often happens that we persecute, and get persecuted by, each other. Throughout the history of the church there have been witch hunts, inquisitions, heresy trials, anathemas, condemnations, and excommunications by those who thought they were offering worship to God. The words of Jesus (Jn 16:3) are as relevant for those Christians who persecute their fellow Christians, from whatever noble motivations, as they are for persecuting unbelievers: They do this because they have not known the Father nor me.

There is, perhaps, some excuse for the unbelievers who persecute Christians, since they know not what they do. In certain cases, this may be true of Christians who persecute their fellow Christians. Still, the latter should really know better.

Saturday of the Fifth Week

Caiaphas as Prophet

Caiaphas says: "It is better...to have one man die for the people than to have the whole nation destroyed." The evangelist adds: "He did not say this on his own, but being high priest that year he prophesied that Jesus was about to die for the nation, and not for the nation only, but to gather into one the dispersed children of God" (Jn 11:49–53).

Caiaphas a prophet?! Well, one may say, there are prophets and there are prophets. There are true prophets and there are false ones. Also, Jesus told us how to tell the difference between the two: "You will know them by their fruits" (Mt 7:15–16). Caiaphas was obviously a false prophet. According to some, the fact that he was removed from the office of high priest about the same time that Pilate was removed as procurator points to some financial arrangement between the two.

However, this may be a little too hasty. What are the fruits produced by the true prophet, as distinguished from the false one? Is the fruit the true prophet produces that of a holy and virtuous life? Or is the fruit the prophecies themselves, the fact that what is prophesied comes to pass? If it is the latter, then Caiaphas prophesied accurately. Further, as with many a prophecy, there is a *sensus plenior* (a fuller sense) implied in what the prophet says. For not only would Jesus die for the nation, as Caiaphas foretold, but he would also die in order to gather into one all of God's children.

Thus, much as we may dislike Caiaphas for his willingness to sacrifice an innocent person upon the altar of political expediency, he was, nonetheless, a true prophet and he prophesied truly.

Palm Sunday

King Jesus of Nazareth

I have always had some difficulty with the feast of Christ the King. First, kings and queens are largely a vanished breed, certainly in terms of real political power. There are no absolute monarchs around these days. Also, such triumphalism seems very much out of place when it comes to the Jesus from Nazareth.

Some Jews in John's gospel voice the objection: "Surely the Messiah is not to come from Galilee!" (7:41). One of Jesus' own future disciples, Nathanael, made the same point: "Can anything good come out of Nazareth?" (Jn 1:46). When it came to kingship, Jesus' background was all wrong.

Granted, he made a triumphal entry into Jerusalem. There were hosannas, cloaks on the road, palm branches, and so forth. But what was he riding? By no stretch of the imagination is a donkey's colt a war-horse, a great white stallion. And yes, he was anointed. But the oil was poured on his feet, not on his head. Further, the one doing the pouring was not a prophet or a priest but, in Luke's gospel (7:37–38), a prostitute.

Finally, what does Jesus do after his triumphal entrance into the Holy City? It was the ideal time to proclaim the messianic kingdom, marshal his followers, take over the temple precincts, seize the day, strike while the iron is hot. And what does Jesus do? As it says in the gospel of Mark (11:11): He went into the temple, looked around at everything, and as it was already late, he went out to Bethany with the twelve. In other words, he walked away. He just walked away.

That is why I have trouble with the feast of Christ the King.

Monday of Holy Week

Judas

Some years back, on an Easter Sunday morning, four of us monks were finishing our coffee, one of the few breakfasts in the year when conversation is permitted. Conversations do take place at breakfast on occasion, but only after the abbot has left. However, that is another story.

Anyway, we were talking about Judas, and trying to figure out why he betrayed his master. We came up with pretty much the same answers that the various gospel accounts do, that is, confusing and conflicting answers.

It is very difficult to know, and judge, the motivations of another. According to John's gospel (12:6), Judas was a thief who stole from the common purse. His motive for handing Jesus over was greed, 30 pieces of silver (Mt 26:15), a paltry sum. Jesus should have commanded a better price. Another was that Judas didn't like being put down by Jesus when he (Judas) suggested that the ointment with which Jesus' feet were anointed might have been sold for a large sum, with the proceeds given to the poor. Still another possibility offered: aware of Jesus' power, Judas wanted to force Jesus' hand and bring on the kingdom right away. Whatever the reason, Judas *did* hand Jesus over, and we really don't know why.

The question is: did Jesus know beforehand that Judas would hand him over to his enemies? If he did, why would he choose someone of whom he would later say, "But woe to him by whom the Son of Man is betrayed. It were better for that man that he had never been born" (Mt 26:24). Would Jesus select someone he knew beforehand would, in despair, go out and hang himself? I think not. When Jesus chose Judas, he picked someone he saw as a good man, someone with promise, who turned out to be a bad choice. If we are human we make bad choices. And Jesus was fully human. So was Judas. It is apparent that Judas made some bad choices along the way, and at least one was very bad.

Which reminds us of the words of St. Paul to the Corinthians: "Let he who stands take heed, lest he fall" (1 Cor 10:12).

Tuesday of Holy Week

Betrayal

"Whoever betrays secrets destroys confidence....Love your friends and keep faith with them; but if you betray their secrets, do not run after them....For a wound may be bandaged, and there is reconciliation after abuse, but whoever has betrayed secrets is without hope." Thus says Sirach (27:16–21).

Jesus picked twelve apostles, and one of them, Judas, betrayed him and handed Jesus over to his enemies.

Betrayal by a friend is really painful. In trusting another with our inmost secrets we entrust to that person our very selves. So when that trust is broken or betrayed, it hurts, it hurts a great deal. This is part of the pain of a divorce. Such a betrayal of trust can even destroy one's ability to trust anyone, ever again.

However, even in such dire situations in our personal lives we know that there is always someone we can trust—one who is eminently and ultimately trustworthy, true, faithful, solid as a rock. Indeed, that is one of the ways the bible describes the person, the personality, if you like, of God, namely with the Hebrew word *emeth*. God is eminently faithful and trustworthy, a fortress in time of trouble.

God never blabs the truth about us. Thank God.

Wednesday of Holy Week

Where Did I Go Wrong?

In the gospel of John, it seems that whenever Jesus goes up to the temple on the occasion of a feast an attempt is made on his life. This would be enough to stop anyone from going to church.

Jesus claims a special relationship with God. In the first place, he calls God Father in a form that is both personal and familiar. Even beyond that, he says that he and the Father are one.

In the gospels, the image exists of Jesus as shepherd. The Father, the eternal shepherd, has given the sheep, the faithful, into Jesus' hands. And no one, not even the Jewish religious leaders, supposedly acting in God's name, can take them out of God's hands. In other words, nothing can frustrate Jesus' purpose, the gift of eternal life for those who believe.

There is a lesson here for us. We must not become overly anxious or discouraged if people, especially those close to us, a son or a daughter, stop practicing their faith or even, apparently, reject it outright. The reasons or excuses usually vary: the position of the "church" on a particular issue, what some priest once said, the boring sermons, the awful music, and so forth. We have to remind ourselves that those given over to Jesus by the Father, the eternal shepherd of the sheep, remain in God's hands. Jesus promises that nothing can frustrate God's purpose of salvation for those the Father has placed in his hands.

Holy Thursday

Washing of Feet

Water was, and is, a precious commodity in the Near East. Yet, giving guests water to wash their feet, or having a servant do the deed, was an important sign of hospitality. Thus, Abraham had water brought so that his three guests under the oaks of Mamre could have their feet washed (Gn 18:4), especially refreshing after a long, hot, and dusty journey. Which was another reason for washing the feet, the practicality of cleansing them from the dust of the road. It is the necessity of being cleansed, wholly cleansed, that Jesus emphasizes at the last supper when he washes the feet of his disciples (Jn 13:1–11).

Getting up in the middle of a meal in order to wash feet was unusual enough, but for the teacher or rabbi to wash his disciples' feet would be most unusual indeed. Simon's reaction was a normal one: "Lord, are you going to wash my feet?"

After washing their feet, Jesus tells his disciples that they are to do the same. We are to cleanse one another of the road dust we pick up on our journey through life. When we see someone down, we are to help them up, dust them off, so that they can be on their way. We are to cleanse and clear the air between those who may be hostile to each other, refresh the spirits of those who are depressed or grieving.

Footwashing comes in various forms. You are meant to use your imagination in figuring out how best to do it.

Good Friday

The Truth

In a court of law, the witness swears that he or she will tell "the truth, the whole truth, and nothing but the truth." Well, that's not quite true. The witness is obligated only to answer the questions posed by the attorneys involved in the case. The witness is not even invited to tell the whole truth, that is, volunteer information not asked for. Indeed, by pleading the Fifth Amendment, the witness is permitted to refuse to tell the truth, if the evidence presented could be self-incriminating.

In the passion narrative in John, Pilate interrogates the witness, Jesus: "Are you the king of the Jews?" (18:33). "What have you done?" (18:35). Jesus' answer is that he came into the world to testify to the truth, and that anyone committed to the truth hears his voice.

"What is truth?" asks Pilate (Jn 18:38). In John's passion narrative Pilate has some of the best lines: "What I have written, I have written" (19:22). Still, that does not mean that we precisely understand his words, anymore than he apparently understood what Jesus meant. A great deal is getting lost in translation. Different languages may be involved, but there is also the problem of different cultures, callings, lifestyles. The world of a Roman governor and that of an itinerant preacher are very different.

The whole procedure, the whole exchange, looked at from Jesus' point of view, could give the appearance of Franz Kafka's *The Trial,* or something from the theater of the absurd. Looked at from God's point of view, however, it all makes sense. And we believe that it makes sense because our very salvation depends upon that truth and upon our belief in that truth.

Pilate asked the right question, and it is the right question: "What is the truth?" He just didn't wait around for the answer.

Holy Saturday

A Quiet Day

Today is one of those quiet days. Not much is happening. Jesus lies in the tomb. In Matthew's account, Joseph of Arimathea had obtained release of Jesus' body, wrapped it in a clean linen shroud, and laid it in his own new tomb (27:57–60). According to the gospel of Luke, the women who had come with Jesus from Galilee saw where Jesus was laid, and are at home preparing spices and ointments (23:55–56). They will rest on the Sabbath. In Mark, on the other hand, Mary Magdalen, Mary the mother of James, and Salome would go out to buy spices only after the Sabbath so that they might come and anoint Jesus' body, giving him a proper Jewish burial (15:42–47). According to John's gospel, however, Jesus had already received more than a proper Jewish burial, at the hands of Nicodemus, a secret disciple, who had accompanied Joseph of Arimathea to the tomb. Nicodemus had brought a mixture of myrrh and aloes, weighing about a hundred pounds—a lavish amount indeed!—and had anointed and wrapped Jesus' body in accordance with Jewish burial customs (19:38–40).

Other than the fact that no one seems to agree precisely what was going on and who was doing what, and when, Jesus was buried and lies in the tomb. It's a quiet day.

It's not exactly the quiet before the storm. The resurrection will not be a storm. There will be no pounding of kettle drums or the fanfare of trumpets. This is not a Hollywood production. The tomb will be quietly emptied of its contents. There will be "Hoorays for God," otherwise known as alleluias. However, they will be quiet ones. After all, it is the Sabbath.

Eventually those alleluias will be heard. We will say them ourselves one day when we follow our Lord and Master, the first born from the dead.

Hooray for God!